THE
OF TH

CW01431101

SIXTY YEARS OF REGENERATION

TONY FLYNN

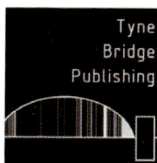

Tyne
Bridge
Publishing

© Tony Flynn 2021

ISBN: 978-1-8382809-4-9

Published by:

City of Newcastle Upon Tyne
Newcastle Libraries
Tyne Bridge Publishing, 2021
unless otherwise indicated
Layout design: Derek Tree

Introduction

This book is a history of the urban redevelopment of Newcastle upon Tyne from the 1960s to the mid-2000s, presented as a walking tour. In the early 1960s, the Leader of the Council T Dan Smith's vision was to make Newcastle 'the Brasilia of the North'; that is, a renewed city, the envy of others. Radical change is inherently divisive, so I leave it up to you to decide whether this plan was successfully implemented.

I was a member of Newcastle City Council from 1980 to 2004. For the first five years of this period, I was a neighbour of T Dan Smith and his local councillor in Spital Tongues, where we had many discussions about the city.

I was the Deputy Leader of the Council under Sir Jeremy Beecham from 1989 to 1994 and Leader of the Council from 1994 to 2004. As leader, I participated in three key decision-making bodies involved in this city's renewal. First, I was a board member of the Tyne and Wear Development Corporation that revitalised the Quayside. Second, I chaired the Grainger Town project that rejuvenated the Georgian town centre. Finally, I was a founding member of the Newcastle and Gateshead Initiative that led the 2008 European Capital of Culture bid. Consequently, I am uniquely placed to narrate the history of the urban regeneration of Newcastle.

The book is based on a walk prepared for the Newcastle City Guides in 2020 for the sixtieth anniversary of the development plans for the city centre. It is designed to be a pocket tour guide with a map in the front identifying the stops. Newcastle is a compact and attractive city. This history is therefore well suited to being presented as a walking tour. The walk starts at the Civic Centre, near the Haymarket Metro Station, and descends down Northumberland Street and Grey Street to the Quayside.

Have a good tour!

This book is dedicated to my wife Barbara, and four children Bridget, Jessica, Jack and Sam, for their love and support.

Tony Flynn

*All the author's royalties from the sale of this book will go to the Newcastle West End Food Bank.

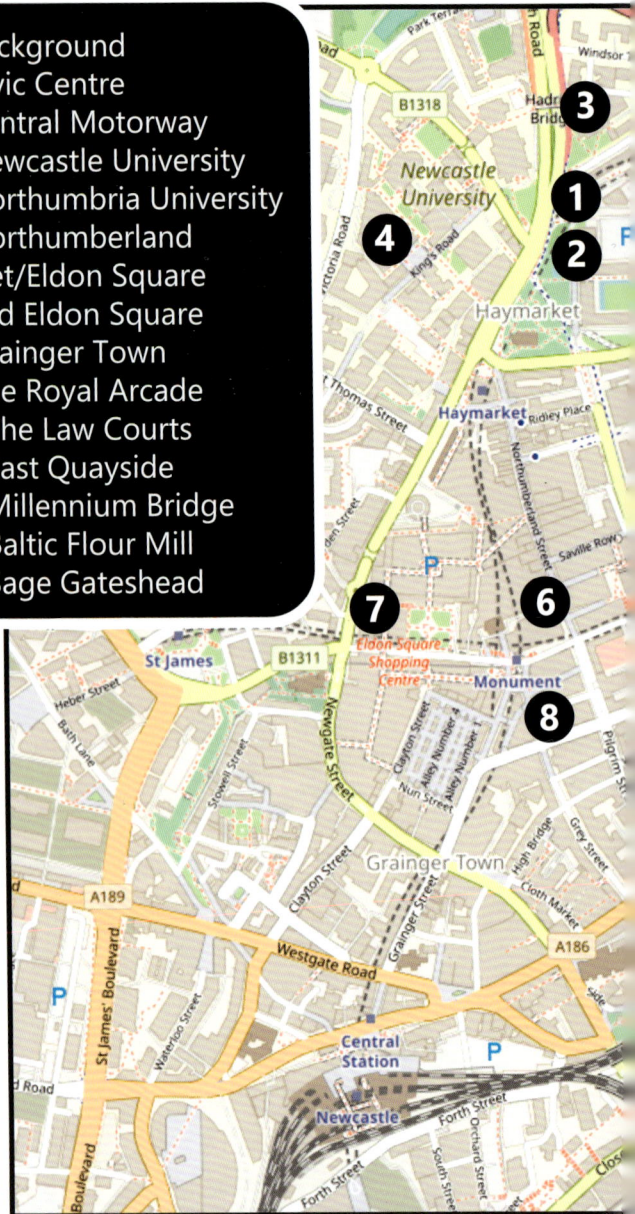

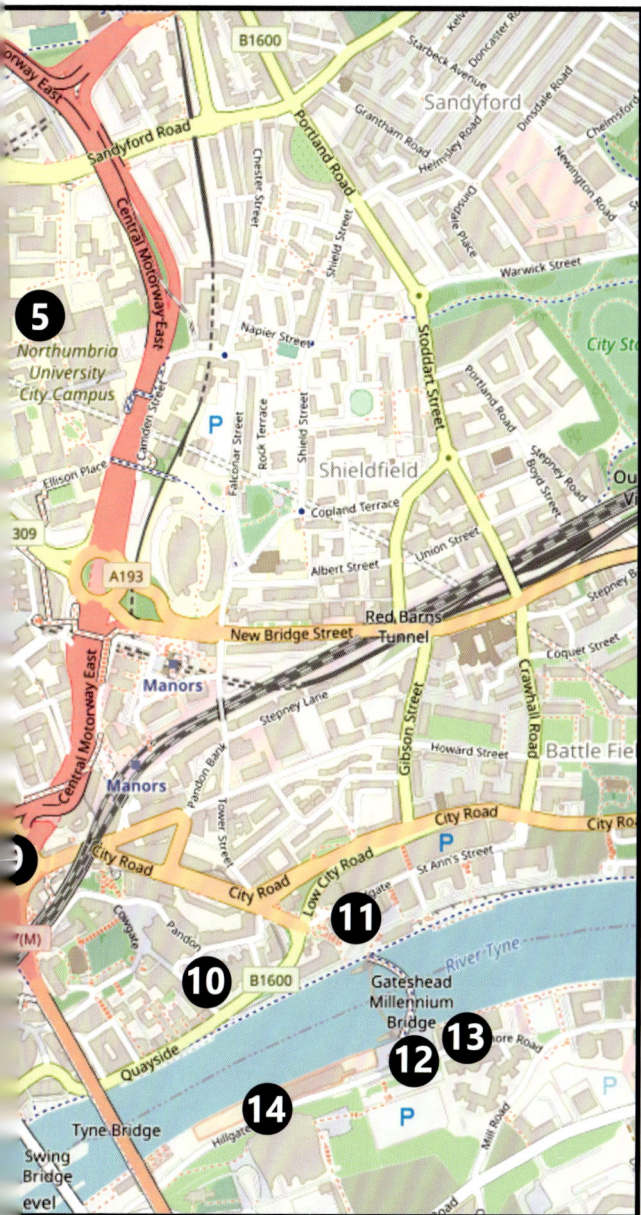

© OpenStreetMap contributor

PLAN OF
NEWCASTLE - UPON - TYNE
1943.

...E OF SLUM CLEARANCE

Newcastle Planning Department in 1955.

A FIVE-YEAR PARTNERSHIP

newCASTLE UPON TYNE

In 1960, T Dan Smith became the Leader of Newcastle City Council. Smith is attributed with the quotation that he intended to transform Newcastle into the "Brasilia of the North", meaning that Newcastle would become a modern city that would be the envy of the world in the same way as Athens or Venice. Perhaps the comparison with Brasilia was an unfortunate one. Brasilia, which became the Capital of Brazil instead of Rio Je Janeiro, was built on a new site without the constraints of a city like Newcastle, which had many buildings of architectural merit. Incidentally, Brasilia had an unusual

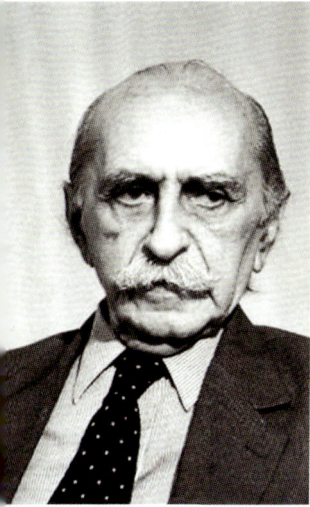

link with Newcastle: the Brazilian architect Lucio Costa, pictured, who was the town planner of Brasilia, was educated at the Royal Grammar School, Newcastle. With hindsight, six decades on from the beginning of the regeneration of the city centre in Newcastle, it is useful to review how various attempts to regenerate Newcastle have fared.

Modern Brasilia

Newcastle in 1946 . Although the city was not as heavily bombed as many other British centres, it was still in the grip of austerity and in need of regeneration.

During the 1950s, Tyneside was experiencing austerity following the Second World War. It was a period of economic and social depression with the decline of traditional industries: coal, shipbuilding and heavy engineering. Newcastle needed to find a new source of wealth, identity and purpose. Car ownership in Britain

Ridley Place, 1964. This image shows how the car began to dominate the city centre.

had massively increased from two million in 1950 to nine million in 1961 and the government-commissioned report by Sir Colin Buchanan "Traffic in Towns" forecast that there would be thirty million cars on the roads by the millennium and that towns would be gridlocked unless something was done about it.

T Dan Smith (pictured) and his recently appointed Director of Planning, Wilfred Burns, turned to the United States of America - where the "car was king" - for inspiration and produced a City Centre Development Plan in 1961 and a Development Plan Review in 1963. Burns had previously worked in

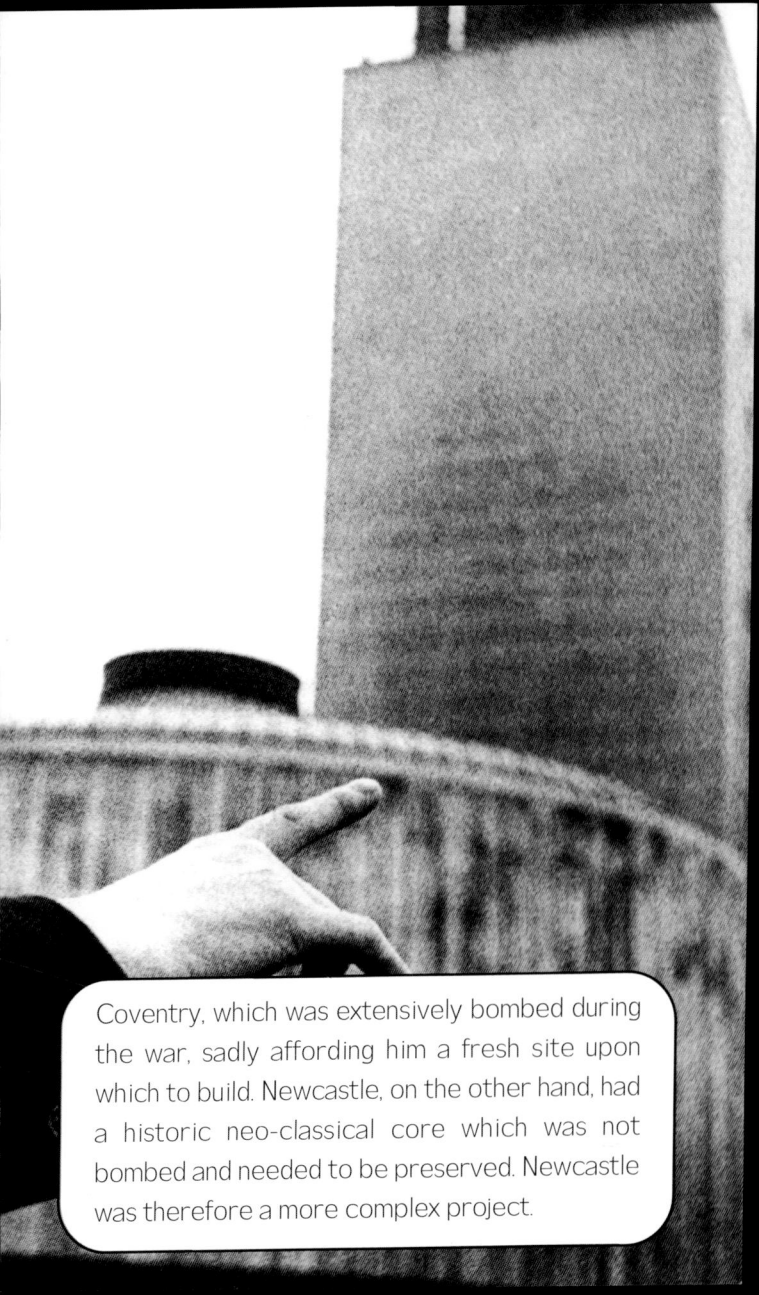

Coventry, which was extensively bombed during the war, sadly affording him a fresh site upon which to build. Newcastle, on the other hand, had a historic neo-classical core which was not bombed and needed to be preserved. Newcastle was therefore a more complex project.

The 1961 and 1963 plans would demolish many of the city's areas of old terraced housing and replace them with blocks of flats. These developments would be connected and supported by an expanded road system, giving priority to traffic movement and separating pedestrians onto walkways. At the same time, the plans sought to conserve historic areas such as Grainger Town. The plans proposed a range of inner-city motorways

Walkways in the sky. Unrealised plans for the Haymarket.

to bypass the core of the city centre. It also recommended an American-style retail mall, the Civic Centre, and an Education Quarter comprising Newcastle University and Newcastle Polytechnic (now Northumbria University). In 1965, T Dan Smith stood down as Leader of the Council after five years in office to become the government-appointed Chair of the

Northern Economic Planning Committee. In 1974 he appeared before Leeds Crown Court for bribery involving the architect John Poulson. Smith pleaded guilty to the charges and was sentenced to six years in prison. Wilfred Burns left Newcastle in 1968 after he was appointed as Chief Planner at the Ministry of Housing and Local Government, becoming Deputy Secretary at the Department of the Environment in 1971. Consequently, only one third of the joint Smith and Burns motorway plan came to fruition before there was a change in direction.

Nevertheless, their short, controversial tenure in office changed Newcastle irrevocably and every redevelopment since has been reaction to those of the 1960s.

River God Tyne at the Civic, by David Wynne

Newcastle Civic Centre is a Grade II listed building designed and built by George Kenyon, the City Architect between 1958 and 1968, and was formally opened by His Majesty King Olav V of Norway on 14th November 1968. It is generally considered to be a remarkable and innovative building. Unlike many buildings of 1960s it was not "Brutalist" in style but was influenced by Scandinavian design, reflecting Newcastle's historic trading links with the region. While work on the building started before T Dan Smith came to power, the bulk of the construction of the Civic Centre occurred during his tenure of office and there is no doubt that he fully supported the lavish artworks as he describes in his 1970 autobiography.

The design of the Civic Centre was conceived as a departure from both the form and the idea of a traditional town hall, which typically had a dominating façade and grand entrance. Instead, the building had a number of separate entrances, symbolising its democratic nature. It was also designed to include function rooms that the general public could hire. The intention was to embrace the people of Newcastle. The building is lavish in design and is unparalleled elsewhere in Britain, where town halls are typically Victorian. It makes a grand statement by employing expensive materials externally and internally, such as Portland Stone and Norwegian Otta Slate as well as a range of marbles and exotic veneers.

The design of the Civic Centre pays homage to Newcastle's medieval and ecclesiastical past. This, together with numerous decorative elements, distinguish it from the modernist architecture of the time. The building plan, with four main blocks grouped around a central lawn, recall the typical monastic layout of a cloister and garth while the carillon tower echoes the bell tower of St Nicholas's Cathedral. The symbolism of the beacon evokes the practice, prevalent during the Middle Ages, of burning a brazier of coals in the lantern of the cathedral, both to help the keelmen navigate the River Tyne and to guide citizens. The splendid Council Chamber and Baronial Banqueting Hall also add to the distinction of the building.

In recent years there has been a reduction in staff working for the local authority due to Government financial cutbacks. The council responded to the cash crisis by upgrading the Civic Centre. This allowed them to lease floor space to other public bodies in order to generate income and preserve this historic building. While there has been controversy about altering the original design by enclosing the arches leading to the Garth, the renovations have generally been received favourably.

Architect George Kenyon at the construction of the Civic Centre in 1966. No expense was spared on quality and the budget of the building was nearly 5 million pounds in 1968, which would be 90 million today.

The Rates Hall in the Civic Centre in 1964 featuring a mural by artist Victor Pasmore, who taught at Newcastle University between 1954 to 1961.

The Civic Centre in 1980 with, below, Swans In Flight by David Wynne.

The Council Chamber and, below, the grand entrance in 1980.

3 CENTRAL MOTORWAY

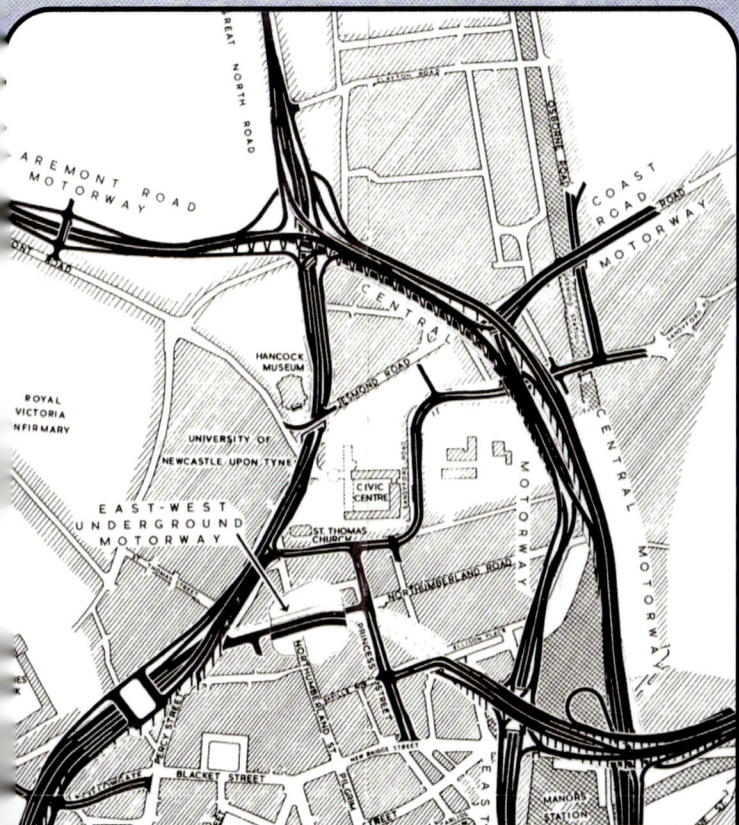

A plan created by City Engineer and Town Surveyor D T Bradshaw, showing how the city would look if the full motorway plan was implemented. In the end, after the Central Motorway was built, it was felt that no more development was necessary.

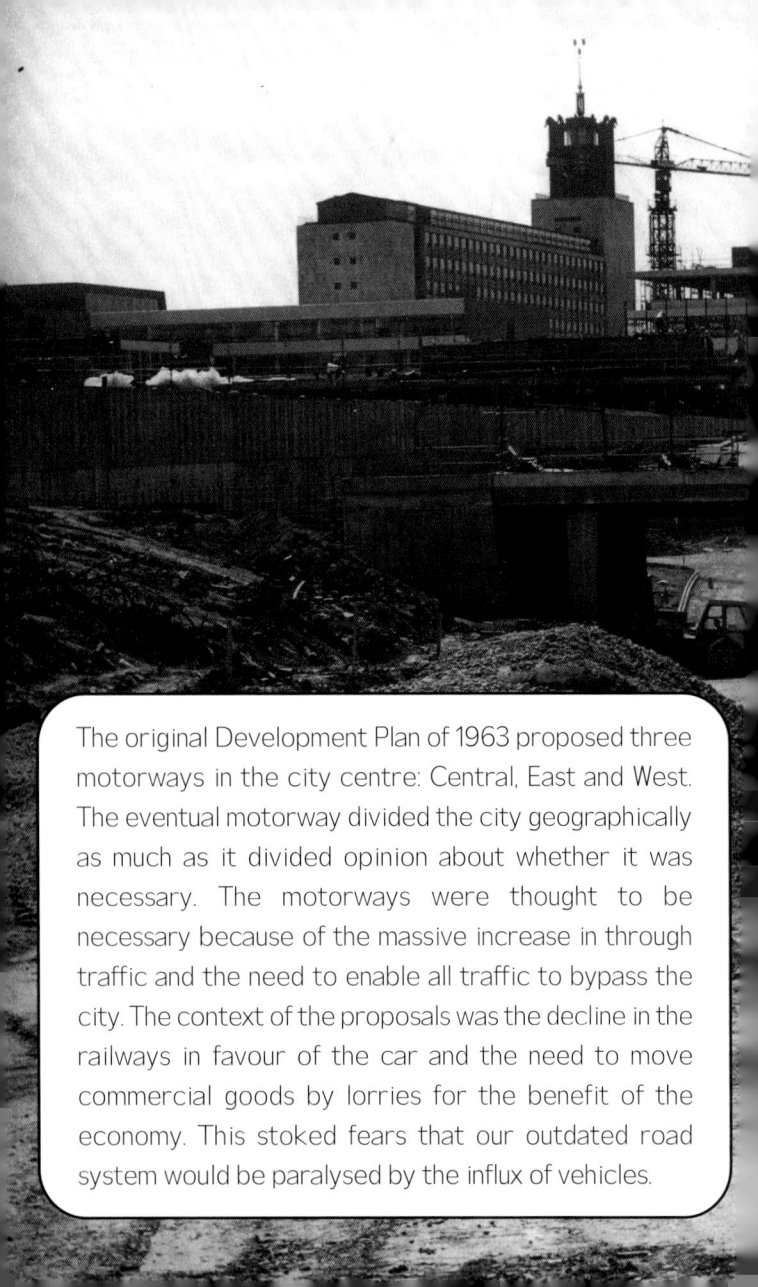

The original Development Plan of 1963 proposed three motorways in the city centre: Central, East and West. The eventual motorway divided the city geographically as much as it divided opinion about whether it was necessary. The motorways were thought to be necessary because of the massive increase in through traffic and the need to enable all traffic to bypass the city. The context of the proposals was the decline in the railways in favour of the car and the need to move commercial goods by lorries for the benefit of the economy. This stoked fears that our outdated road system would be paralysed by the influx of vehicles.

Construction of the Central Motorway before its completion in 1973.

However, only the Central Motorway – completed in 1973 – was delivered. Once the central motorway had been built, a growing number of people felt it had achieved the objective of protecting the city and that no other motorways were desirable or necessary. The east and west motorways were rejected because of environmental concerns and emerging plans to build a Metro (light transit system) to meet the city's transport needs. If all three of the proposed motorways had been built, the centre of the city would have looked like a concrete jungle with motorways zig-zagging around the central core, like "Spaghetti Junction" in Birmingham, alongside futuristic "walkways in the sky". It would have been a city for cars rather than for pedestrians. The central motorway allowed traffic for the first time to bypass the City Centre.

The planned road system was controversial, especially in the middle-class suburb of Jesmond, where the motorway would have required land from parks, school playing fields, and existing homes. Local residents formed an environmental group, Save our City from Environmental Mess or SOC'EM. The group was not an example of nimbyism ('not in my back yard'), opposing the development of urban motorways, it was also concerned about the destruction of the historic city centre: for example, the Old Eldon Square.

The height of SOC'EM's success occurred in 1972 when the City Council, then under Conservative control, held consultations regarding further motorway plans. SOC'EM launched an aggressive campaign opposing the plans and employed their own planning and transport experts. Although the council ultimately passed the plans, the Secretary of State for the Environment, Peter Walker, questioned the wisdom of the scheme and responded by stating he would only approve the plans if there were a radical rethink. The city council at this point abandoned the East Motorway.

In 1975, the Secretary of State, Bill Rogers, gave the go-ahead for the Metro after the Tyne and Wear Council was formed between 1974 and 1986. The council was determined to introduce a comprehensive Metro scheme throughout the region as an alternative priority for transport to motorways.

CHANGING NEWCASTLE

THE IMPACT OF MODERN DEVELOPMENT ON THE CITY CENTRE

a town trail

SOC'EM!
Save Our City from Environmental Mess !

Newcastle University, 1965.

Newcastle University has its origins in the School of
Medicine and Surgery, established in 1834, as well as the
Armstrong building founded in 1871. These two colleges
formed one division of the University of Durham and

were merged to form King's College in 1937. In 1963, King's College became Newcastle University. Following a national expansion in higher education, Newcastle University now boasts 25,000 students.

Design sketch for what would become the Claremont Road development, an important part the university's 1960s expansion. Below, The Centre for Life.

T Dan Smith and the city council played a major role in securing the university's independent status. The council bought land and lobbied the Government to secure the university's presence on a single site in the city centre to form an Education Quarter with the polytechnic sited at the other side of the Civic Centre. The educational developments were later complemented by a cultural strategy that breathed new life into the city's arts establishments. The vision was a city centre that buzzed with shoppers and office workers during the day, while providing central living accommodation for students and local residents - bringing the city to life in the evening.

In 1994, I succeeded Lord Jeremy Beecham as Leader of Newcastle Council. In conjunction with the Tyne and Wear Development Corporation, we worked with the university to secure finance from the Millennium Commission and the National Lottery for the Centre for Life site for the Genetics Institute as the city's Millennium Project. Similarly, when Scottish and Newcastle Breweries announced that they were to move their bottling plant out of the city, the council secured the important city centre site in partnership with the university and One North East, the Regional Development Agency, to invest in what has become Helix, the science campus of the university. This has allowed the university to further expand within the city centre.

The Catalyst, left, and the Urban Sciences Building are just two of the new landmarks that make up Helix, the science campus of the university

In 2002, the university – through one of its ex students Sir Terry Farrell – produced a "Master Plan" for its city centre site. The plan sought to connect the university more closely to the city, with an emphasis on pedestrian routes and new quadrangles within the campus and reduced spaces for cars at the fringes of the site. The new King's Gate Student and Administrative site helps define the university with an attractive frontage looking out to the Civic Centre.

Newcastle has a reputation as one of the most popular university cities because of its central location and identity with city life. A relatively high proportion of former students remain in the city after graduation, adding to the vitality and economy of the city. The vision in the 1960s Council Development Plan of higher education being at the centre of the city's regeneration plans has been a real success.

Architect and ex-Newcastle student Sir Terry Farrell on the day he graduated.

Northumbria University, to the east of the Civic Centre has its origins in three colleges: Rutherford College of Technology, the College of Art and Industrial Design and the Municipal College of Commerce. In 1969, the three colleges were amalgamated to form Newcastle Polytechnic under the direction of the city council. The polytechnic became the major regional centre for the training of teachers with the creation of the City's College of Education in 1974 and Northern Counties

Northumbria University's Computer and Information Sciences building.

Colleges for Education in 1976. In 1992, Newcastle Polytechnic was reconstituted as the Northumbria University as part of a nationwide process in which polytechnics became universities.

Northumbria University has had very close links with the city council over many years. Council members have served on its Board of Governors and the university gained the council's support in expanding its city centre campus across the Central Motorway to a new site by way of an attractive bridge. The university is one of the high-ranking former polytechnics and attracts the same number of students as Newcastle University.

Since 2000, the university has consolidated its presence on two major campuses in Newcastle: one in the city centre and the other in a suburban location on the edge of the city at Coach Lane. There has been major landscaping and the removal of cars on the city centre campus.

The university has been keen to identify itself with the city centre location to attract students. This led to a naming dispute with Newcastle University when it rebranded itself as Northumbria University Newcastle.

Students outside their library.

It was probably unthinkable for the council leaders in the 1960s to imagine that the two universities today would lead to a student population of over 55,000 in the city, making such an invaluable contribution in every area of life. The council's foresight has reaped huge dividends for the city.

Northumbria Students' Union.

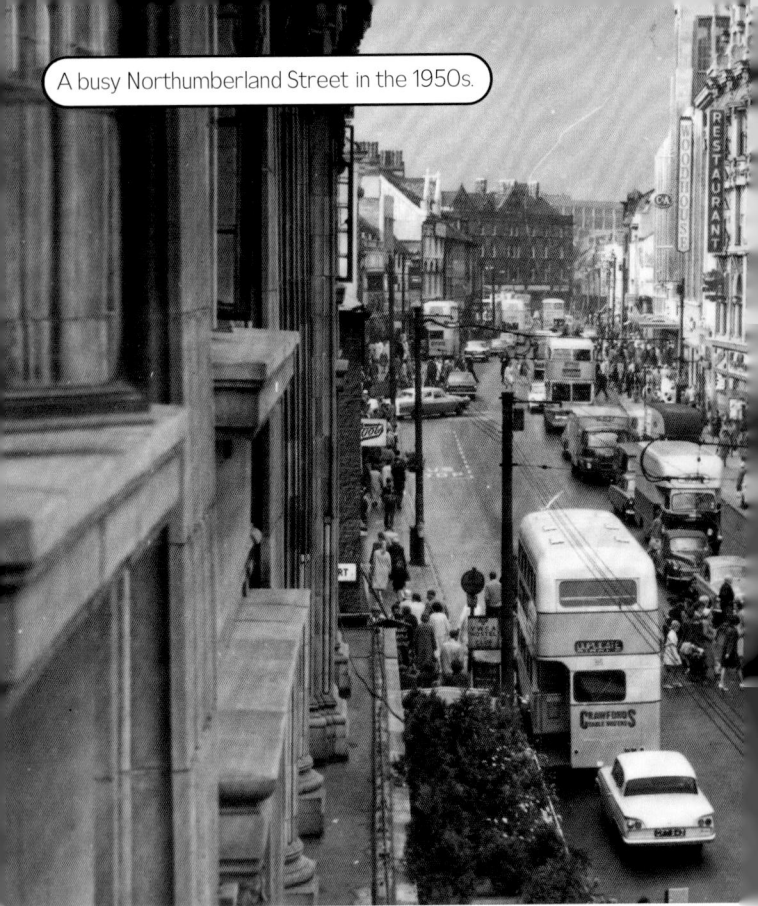

A busy Northumberland Street in the 1950s.

Between the construction of the Tyne Bridge in 1928 and the opening of the Tyne Tunnel in 1967, Northumberland Street was part of the A1, the major road between London and Edinburgh. Photographs from the 1960s onward portray Northumberland Street as a clustered street with pedestrian shoppers "taking their

lives in their hands", crossing the busy street to avoid vehicles. Pedestrian bridges were built to provide alternative routes for shoppers to avoid the mayhem. The opening of the Central Motorway in 1973 removed much of the through traffic. From 1999 onwards, Northumberland Street has become pedestrianised.

The site of Eldon Square Shopping Centre, 1973

In 1976, the American-style retail mall, Eldon Square indoor shopping centre, opened with 156 new shopping units drawing large numbers of visitors from around the region. Four years later, the Tyne and Wear Metro system opened, making it much easier for shoppers to

travel into town. The volume of traffic was further reduced in 1980 when the Western Bypass through Gateshead was opened, taking traffic west and north away from the city centre. The reduced through traffic allowed the city to become more pedestrian-friendly.

Design for Eldon Square and, opposite, the resulting interior in 1982.

In the 1980s, the final decision was taken not to build the western motorway that would have brought the road over Redheuth Bridge to Gallowgate and plunged it down to the Haymarket. Instead, a two-lane carriageway, St James's Boulevard was built, along with the widening of Barrack Road to take traffic away from the city centre. The new gateway to the city gave a magnificent view of the iconic St James Park (left).

The ease of access to Northumberland Street and the positive visitor experience has enabled Eldon Square shopping centre to thrive, despite the competition following the opening, in 1986, of the Metrocentre shopping centre, outside of Gateshead town centre, which despite its name cannot be accessed by the light transit system.

Opposite page, The construction of the Metro at Monument in 1977. An information leaflet on the Metro system from 1981.

The success of Northumberland Street has been achieved through the foresight of the political leaders in the 1960s, who sadly recognised manufacturing jobs had already been lost and that the city's economy would recover as a regional capital through the expansion of the higher education sector, local government, the retail and service sector rather than traditional manufacturing. The city council has also benefited financially from its 40% stake in Eldon Square that contributes 7 million pounds annually to the council budget. Unlike the Metrocentre, Eldon Square shopping centre is enhanced as it leads onto traditional shops in Northumberland Street. The Metro system, Eldon Square shopping centre, pedestrianisation, and the Central Motorway bypass have all contributed to the success of Northumberland Street.

The planned shopping centre, Eldon Square, opened in 1976. It was built on the site of what is now known as Old Eldon Square, which was constructed in 1825 in a neo-classical style designed by John Dobson, the famous north east architect. It was named after John Scott, who was born the son of a coal merchant on Newcastle's Quayside and was elevated to become Lord Eldon, Lord Chancellor of England, the chief legal officer in the country.

It is generally thought to be a masterpiece of Georgian architecture. At the beginning of the 1960s, it was in a run-down state and the council believed that it should be demolished to make way for what would, ironically, be named Eldon Square shopping centre. Demolishing part of Old Eldon Square appeared to be progressive and enlightened to some in the early 1960s but seemed insensitive, brutal and philistine to groups such as SOC'EM by the time it came to be demolished.

A sketch of Eldon Square c1840.

The Eldon Centre Plan was to knock down Old Eldon Square and replace it with a modern development. The Danish architect, Arne Jacobsen, was commissioned to build a 28-storey hotel as the centrepiece of the new shopping complex. However, the plan for the hotel was scrapped in 1970 for economic reasons and the space was replaced with a bland, faceless high brick wall. The exterior overlooking the square has been substituted recently with a more outward looking development and a new entrance and pathways linking the two parts of Eldon Square across Blackett Street.

The green in front of Eldon Square has for a long time been a meeting place for young people. In the late 1960s, it gained the name "Hippie Green" following the "flower power" revolution. In the 1980s, it became a meeting place for goths. Now that Eldon Square has become a major thoroughfare, it is more generally used by the wider public.

Old Eldon Square could have been restored to its former glory in recent years. Its demolition was seen as an act of vandalism by some and galvanised many to oppose further destruction of Newcastle's historic core. Demands for conservation eventually led to the restoration of Richard Grainger's classical town centre.

Between 1834 and 1840, the Newcastle-born developer, Richard Grainger, below, built the first residential and commercial town centre in the country in a neo-classical style. The Grainger Town Regeneration Project that took place from 1997 to 2003 restored the historic core of Newcastle to original grandeur after many years of economic decline and physical

decay. In the 1970s, retail in the Grainger Town declined as the shops moved northwards to Eldon Square and nearer to the new metro system. For example, during this period the department store Bainbridge's relocated from Grainger Town to Eldon Square, leaving a derelict property. Sir Jeremy Beecham was the Leader of Council from 1977 to 1994 and he began the restoration of Grainger Town through the use of government money from the Inner City Partnership to clean the soot-ridden

Grainger Street around 1900 and, inset, Richard Grainger.

buildings and restore their golden sandstone appearance. In the 1980s and the 1990s, offices moved to the out-of-town business parks and the regenerated Quayside, where on-site parking was guaranteed. As a result, Grainger Town was in decline with over half of its Grade I and II listed buildings at risk of collapse. By the 1990s, Grainger Town had a million square feet of empty office space. In some cases, buildings had been empty for over 25 years and were at the mercy of the elements, with trees growing out of the brickwork and damp and dry rot inside of the buildings. One infamous building was numbers 2 to 12 Grey Street. Over a six-year period 360 million pounds was spent restoring the area with council and government money leading the way, but for every pound spent by the public sector, six pounds was invested by the private sector as they recognised it was money well spent as the area was again "on the up".

A dedicated regeneration team was established, working out of the Central Exchange building between 1997 and 2003. A management board – chaired by myself in my capacity as the Leader of Council (1994 to 2004) – was instituted. The board involved the private sector and residents with the principal aim of bringing confidence back to the area by restoring the heart of the city. One of the problems in Grainger Town was

2 to 12 Grey Street, before and after restoration.

coping with Grainger's legacy. While his development in the centre of the town was very successful, his subsequent development in the west end of the town at Elswick was a failure, and would have bankrupted him if it were not for his friend and mentor John Clayton, the Town Clerk. Clayton managed to stave off the creditors and kept Grainger's reputation intact by nimble financial manoeuvring. Although Grainger died heavily in debt in 1861, his solicitors managed to keep the estate intact until 1901. However, at this point it was divided up among many owners, which meant that it was difficult to gain agreement for a comprehensive redevelopment, leading to a hotchpotch of interventions undermining the impact of the grand design.

One of the major tasks for the Grainger Town project was to discover property ownership and then to encourage the owners to invest in the area with grants and a vision. This was initially achieved by investment in the public realm that involved the cleaning and lighting of the sandstone buildings, encouraging pedestrian spaces and laying high-quality Caithness stone from Scotland, the original stone of the town.

The Theatre Royal.

Grey's Monument looks down over modern day Grainger Town.

Royal Arcade, 1833.

Royal Arcade, 1958.

The Royal Arcade was built to a design by John Dobson on the site of the present-day Swan House between 1831 and 1832. At the time, it was akin to modern shopping centres such as Eldon Square in that it housed not only shops but also offices and other amenities: banks, auction rooms, a post office, as well as a steam and vapour bath. The interior of the arcade was floored with chequered stone and black marble and lit by eight conical skylights set in domes high up in the roof. There were eight shops on either side of the mall.

Unfortunately, the building was poorly sited and never became the commercial success it might have been. Only the western entrances opened towards the town centre, which was some distance away. The success of the arcade was not helped by the opening of shops in Grey Street and Grainger Street that diverted trade away from it.

The Royal Arcade began to decline as a shopping centre and was left to decay until there was a decision to demolish it in 1963 to make way for Swan House, based on a roundabout in the middle of the Central Motorway system. During demolition, every piece of stonework was numbered with paint, the intention being to rebuild the arcade in front of Swan House. The pieces were stored on various outdoor sites and it was not long before the numbers had washed off, Tyneside weather being what it is. What remains is a replica of the inside of the old arcade, which actually cost 45,000 pounds to build - more than the original.

Swan House replaced the Royal Arcade and was named after Joseph Swan, the chemist who worked nearby in Mosley Street and invented one of the first electric light bulbs in 1878. There is an ongoing debate about whether Swan House is a landmark building or an eyesore. As you enter the city over the Tyne Bridge, it is the first building you see, dominating the horizon. Some have condemned it as a monument to 1960s "Brutalist" architecture.

Swan House became the headquarters of the Post Office and then British Telecom. When the latter vacated the building, it was renamed 55 Degrees North, after the earth's circle of latitude that runs through the city, and to remove the negative connotations. In 2002, the building was converted into executive apartments that have a birds-eye view of the city.

The Royal Arcade, like Old Eldon Square, was demolished as a result of what conservationists believed to be vandalism. The outcry against these decisions contributed to the growing demand to conserve the historic core of Grainger's classical town and stop further motorway expansion.

Swan House in 1972.

As part of the regeneration of the Quayside, the Newcastle Law Courts opened in 1990. The building of the courts on the Quayside was an act of faith on behalf of the local authority in restoring the riverside after many years of decline. The loss of coal mining and associated industries had resulted in the city turning its back on the river where its wealth had been created. The belief was that if Newcastle returned its focus to the riverside its wealth would be restored.

In 1929, the Tyne Bridge was built to create employment for local people during the depression. However, the building of the bridge had the unintended consequence of further increasing the decline of the Quayside as traffic was diverted from the riverside to the north of the city.

An unfinished walkway to the Quayside.

The Tyne Bridge at the begining of the 1960s bringing in increased traffic.

During the 1960s, Newcastle Council considered the demolition of much of the Quayside apart from the Guildhall, the Custom's House, Trinity House and All Saint's Church. The proposal was to replace it with stone-faced buildings, similar to those at St Cuthbert and St Bede House (pictured), built around Swan House with walkways descending to the Quayside. This redevelopment thankfully halted in midair.

In the early 1970s, the River Authority produced a report stating that, after generations of industrial activity, the Tyne was heavily polluted and putrid as 270 sewers poured 35 million gallons of sewerage into the river annually. A ten-year investment plan was put in place, providing an interceptor sewer to Howden for water treatment, making the Tyne a fine salmon river again.

The potential of the Quayside area as somewhere that was attractive rather than to be avoided slowly became apparent. In 1986, the city attracted the first of three Tall Ships races to Newcastle that began to change the public's perception of the riverside as a place of beauty. In 1998, the Angel of the North sculpture by Anthony Gormley was erected in Gateshead, attracting worldwide media attention.

In response to the demise of traditional industries in the major conurbations, the Government set up the Tyne and Wear Development Corporation with Alastair Balls as Chief Executive to regenerate the north east riverside areas. In Newcastle this principally meant East Quayside. The Corporation was a government-appointed body that was given local planning powers taken from local authorities to produce a ten-year plan to spend public money exclusively developing run-down areas. The Urban Development Corporation (UDC) had Government appointed representatives from the public and private sector including, on Tyneside, three local authorities, although Gateshead chose not to be a part of the UDC area, preferring to redevelop their land themselves. A master plan for the Quayside was drawn up by the locally-educated architect Sir Terry Farrell that removed the rundown Quayside sheds and planned a mix-use development including housing, leisure and office facilities with rear car parking. The beauty of the scheme was that it gave priority to pedestrians along riverside walkways, with office buildings set back from the quay, designed by different architects but working to the same proportions set down in the overall plan.

A rundown Quayside in 1980.

The success of East Quayside led to the development in Gateshead Quays. The successful mix-use development of work, leisure and housing encouraged visitors to promenade along the revitalised riverside and made it a major tourist attraction. The redevelopment of East Quayside encouraged Gateshead Council to complement this development on the South Bank of the river with a

culture-led regeneration strategy with land it had purchased. Gateshead Council was able to secure the largest amount of money from the National Lottery up to that point to contribute to the building of the Gateshead Millennium Bridge that linked both sides of the river, the Baltic Centre for Contemporary Art and the Sage music centre, cultural facilities that are discussed later.

Newcastle and Gateshead's Partnership.

In 1998 Newcastle Council dissolved the Newcastle Initiative: a marketing organisation for the city. Instead, the Newcastle and Gateshead Initiative (NGI) was established in 2000, with the aim of promoting both conurbations in partnership. The Journal newspaper announced the partnership describing the councils as "burying their traditional hatchets" to usher in a "new era of cooperation". One of NGI's most important roles was

to spearhead Newcastle and Gateshead's joint bid to become European Capital of Culture in 2008. Despite being the bookies' favourite, Liverpool was awarded this title by an independent body in 2003. Despite the huge disappointment, the NGI pursued their ten-year programme of cultural regeneration that made it the cultural capital it is today, creating a lasting renaissance. NGI is a flourishing organisation today and of course supports the City Guides in achieving our successful walks and tours.

Work in progress, 1997.

Gateshead Council's strategy was to develop a Cultural Quarter on the South Bank of the Tyne and to achieve maximum success it proposed a new pedestrian and cycle bridge to link both communities. In 1996 Gateshead Council held a design competition for an attractive bridge for their Millennium Project, with the intention of applying for funding from the Millennium Commission. The competition was won by the consulting engineers Gifford and Partners and the architects Wilkinson Eyre. In 1997 the Millennium Commission awarded Gateshead 9.4 million pounds, amounting to roughly half the building costs of the new bridge.

At full tilt - it was the first bridge to win the prestigious R.I.B.A Stirling Prize for Architecture in 2003 and, opposite, being put in place in 2000 by one of the world's largest floating cranes, the mighty Asian Hercules II.

The unique tilting design of the bridge was a world first. The Millennium Bridge opens by means of turning the walkway on hydraulically powered pivots within the concrete bases on each side of the Tyne. As the arch of the bridge lowers to open, the deck rises to an angle of 40 degrees, allowing ships to sail beneath. The bridge provides a navigational channel of thirty metres, equal to the Swing Bridge, and a headroom clearance (when open) of twenty five metres, equal to the Tyne Bridge. The movement of the bridge can be compared to the opening and closing of a huge eyelid, similar to a blinking eye. Each opening and closing of the bridge takes four minutes and is powered by electricity. In 2014, this reportedly cost 10 pounds to open and shut, discounting the cost of staff wages. A computer-controlled coloured lighting system ensures the bridge looks spectacular at night.

Asian Hercules II

On 20th November 2000 one of the world's largest floating cranes, Asian Hercules II, caused huge excitement when it arrived to lift the bridge into position. Nothing had been seen like it before on Tyneside and interest was intense. Many thousands gathered to witness the event, while millions followed the event on worldwide television. On 17th September 2001, the Gateshead Millennium Bridge was formally opened by the Queen and became a world-famous landmark overnight, complementing the six other bridges across the Tyne gorge.

Above, the bridge today, and below Sir Bobby Robson celebrates the millennium with Tony Flynn, right, and, Mick Henry, of Gateshead Council.

The Baltic Centre for Contemporary Art was the second major development on the south bank of the river and it was where the renewal of Gateshead's Quays really started. The Baltic Flour Mill opened in 1950. Its owners were Joseph Rank Ltd who named their mills after seas. The mill was only open for thirty years, closing in 1981. The Baltic is situated on the river's edge, where imported grain was poured into large silos and then transferred into a mill to be ground into flour. The mill was demolished in the 1980s but the silo element remained and was regenerated as an art gallery in 2002.

The Baltic reflects three late 20th-century international trends: culture-led regeneration, the reclamation of industrial sites especially on waterfronts, and the transformation of large industrial buildings for art spaces. The Baltic was converted between 1998 and 2002 by Ellis Williams Architects.

The Baltic is a new type of highly flexible public art venue; an "art factory" rather than a gallery with a permanent collection. It has six main floors with three mezzanines. The Baltic provides galleries, studios, a cinema, lecture theatre, a library and an archive. The inside was stripped of its silos and the east and west walls replaced with glass, while a top-floor restaurant was created. It has two outside lifts that complement the inside stairwell. There are two viewing platforms

The Baltic Flour Mill in the 1950s.   Photo: James Allan

with amazing panoramic views. A gallery entrance with a bookshop and restaurant leads outside to a piazza that overlooks the river. The Turner Prize was held at this venue in 2011, which was the first time it was held outside of London.

The Baltic is a wonderful building that houses challenging art and as there is free entrance the gallery attracts a large number of visitors.

14 SAGE GATESHEAD

The Sage was the third and final development on Gateshead Quays that completed its designation as a cultural quarter. It is named after its principal sponsor, the computer software company Sage. The building opened in 2004 and the architects were Norman Foster & Partners. The venue was largely funded through Arts Lottery. The building houses two concert halls, rehearsal spaces and community learning facilities. The roof envelope overhangs the self contained concert halls that are wrapped around with tiers of walkways with outside views. The Sage provides a permanent home for the Royal Northern Sinfonia and Folkworks, a traditional music and dance organisation. The purpose-built timber lined main auditorium is designed to provide the best acoustics.

The Sage is a marvelous place to relax, enjoy music, and take in the spectacular views of the Quayside. There is an artwork called the "Ribbon of Glass" by Kate Maestri that runs from the outside of the building through the concourse. A piazza leads to the principal entrance with reception areas, café, restaurant, shop and concourse. There is free entry with access to many parts of the building and internal tours of the halls.

Conclusion

NewcastleGateshead has evolved over the last sixty years into an attractive cosmopolitan destination. In the 1960s, following post-war austerity and the decline in traditional industries, the municipal vision was to create the "Brasilia of the North" and transform the town into a modern city giving priority to the car. The 1961 City Development Plan was very much a product of its time and has been justifiably criticised since. Only a third of the planned motorway developments were built and public pressure prevented the town been dominated by the car.

While most people now accept that the Central Motorway was necessary, thankfully the Motorway East and West were not built, allowing the Metro to become the preferred method of transporting passengers into town, enabling Northumberland Street to become pedestrianised. Opposition to motorway developments from SOC'EM challenged the uncontrolled power of city planners and prevented a "halter of roads" being placed around the city's neck that would have choked life, instead allowing architectural conservation to flourish.

Fortunately, the city centre as it now is very much a compromise of what it might have been under Smith and Burns's original plans. The destruction of Old Eldon Square and the Royal Arcade led to a demand for the conservation of historic buildings and the regeneration of Grainger Town. The positive council decision to build

Eldon Square Shopping Centre in Northumberland Street has helped preserve the city centre, unlike out-of-town shopping centres elsewhere that have killed the towns.

The Development Plan's vision to build an Education Quarter in the city centre with Newcastle University and later Northumbria University at either side of the newly built Civic Centre has led to a collective undergraduate population of 55,000. Drawing people into the city centre was a key part of the plan. The place now buzzes with shoppers and office workers by day while providing central living accommodation

for locals and students who bring the city centre to life at night. The restoration of Grainger Town and its link to the renovated Quayside and the Cultural Quarter in Gateshead has produced a partnership between the two councils that is unrivalled in this country.

The attractiveness of the compact city has encouraged international visitors to this premier tourist destination. Today we rightly celebrate the transformation of NewcastleGateshead from a giant of the Industrial Revolution to a regional and cultural capital that is second to none!

Photo Credits

Many thanks to the following for allowing Tyne Bridge Publishing to use their photographs:

Evening Chronicle: Page 14, 15, T Dan Smith.
Malcolm Maybury: 1997 Quayside photograph.
Steve Brock: Modern photograph of river at night, Northumberland Street, Northumberian University p46 and p49.
Steve Ellwood: Modern photographs of Civic Centre, The Baltic, The Sage, Millennium Bridge p96 & p98, Newcastle University p36, Northumbria University p44 and unfinished walkway.
www.eccentricsleevenotes.com: People on Eldon Green
Sir Terry Farrell: Terry Farrell photograph.
Tom Yellowley: Modern photographs of Old Eldon Square, the Monument, Grainger Town and East Quayside.
Ward Philipson Photo Memories: Royal Arcade photo.
Eldon Square: Interior of Eldon Square.
Jack Flynn: Portrait of author.

All other photographs are the copyright of Newcastle Libraries or Derek Tree.

The map in this book used data which is available under the Open Database License. See openstreetmap.org for more information.